Oral History
AS A TEACHING APPROACH
by John A. Neuenschwander

National Education Association
Washington, D.C.

Acknowledgments

The manuscript has been reviewed by Helen M. Ed-
monston, retired social studies teacher, Montgomery
County (Maryland) Public Schools and Alice Hoffman,
Oral History Association.

Library of Congress Cataloging in Publication Data

Neuenschwander, John A.
    Oral history as a teaching approach.

    (Developments in classroom instruction)
    Bibliography: p.
    1. Oral history.   2. Interviewing.   I. Title.
II. Series.
D16.N47   907'.2   75-23013
ISBN 0-8106-1801-X

ORAL HISTORY
as a Teaching Approach

CONTENTS

1. Background

In the last fifteen years the field of oral history has experienced tremendous growth. The practice of interviewing individuals on tape about their life and times in order to collect valuable source material is now a well-established field in its own right. There are currently over four hundred oral history projects across the country ranging in size from the massive collection at Columbia University to very small projects like the one in Wauwatosa, Wisconsin, with a handful of volunteers and lots of enthusiasm.[11] In addition, there are a number of programs in Canada and Great Britain. The immense popularity of books based on oral history like *The Foxfire Book*, *Plain Speaking*, and *Working* is a good indication that stories straight from the lips of elderly Americans have made the past come alive for millions of readers.

Oral history is also becoming an increasingly important teaching tool. While its use in teaching is still far overshadowed by the research application, a recent nationwide survey conducted by the Oral History Association indicates that it may well become one of the most significant new teaching approaches of the 1970's. A sampling of comments from the teachers who responded to this survey underscores this point:

> Oral History has really added a lot to our American Studies program. The community is interested and students have participated so well.
>
> Marjorie Woodard, Oswego High School,
> Oswego, Illinois

> There are still many possible areas for use of the oral history technique which we have not begun to explore.
>
> Betty Jean Southard, Schaumburg High School,
> Schaumburg, Illinois

7

> It lurches, it breaks down, it doesn't always corner well, it is tied together with bailing wire in places, but [expletive deleted], it is on the road and running.[13]
>
> Edward Ives, University of Maine, Orono, Maine

The field of oral history is both ancient and modern. While historians since Herodotus have been interviewing individuals about significant historical events, it was not until the late 1940's that Allan Nevins truly modernized the historical interview. By joining together the interview techniques of the social sciences, a tape recorder, and the historian's perspective, Professor Nevins established an Oral History Research Office at Columbia University. The initial purpose of the program was to interview prominent Americans about their role in and observations on American history and life. In this way he hoped to counter the alarming loss of valuable source materials caused by technological wonders such as the telephone.[5] During the 1950's oral history made steady but unspectacular progress. By the mid-1960's, however, the practice of oral history had become so widespread that a national organization was founded to promote and develop the technique. The presence of archivists, librarians, physicians, social scientists, assorted laypersons, and historians at each of these annual national colloquia beginning in 1966 is an indication of the truly interdisciplinary nature of oral history.[8]

In addition to the creation of a national organization in the 1960's, a noticeable shift took place in the types of individuals being interviewed. While some of the earlier programs affiliated with large universities and Presidential libraries continued to concentrate on prominent national and regional figures, many rapidly emerging projects at the grass roots level were beginning to seek out representatives of ethnic, minority, and regional sub-culture groups. The creation of oral history programs on the county and community levels also helped to lay the groundwork for the development of oral history as a teaching tool. The first attempts to involve students in oral history were often undertaken by teachers who, through participation in a local project, had become aware of the human resources in their own communities.

The most successful use of oral history in teaching thus far is the Foxfire Project. Here, Eliot Wigginton, a young English teacher at Rabun Gap-Nacoochee High School in Georgia, initiated a community-centered oral history project in hopes of stimulating his students.[16] The first tangible result was a student magazine called *Foxfire*. The instant popularity of this enchanting periodical about the culture of southern Appalachia resulted in the publication of an anthology. From the accounts of faithhealing and log cabin building to the observations by such local savants as Aunt Arie, *The Foxfire Book* is a superb illustration of integrative social studies. As Reed Whittemore noted in a recent book review, "What began as a casual exercise in improving student motivation has emerged as a positive pedagogical device for learning itself . . . ."[15]

Despite the sale of over three hundred thousand copies of *The Foxfire Book* and the recent publication of a second anthology, the use of oral history in teaching has yet to become widespread. The concentration of the Oral History Association on the research application is perhaps one contributing factor. Ironically, the overwhelming success of the Foxfire Project itself may have actually been a deterrent as well. In any event the work of Eliot Wigginton has served to underscore the tremendous educational potential of oral history.

It is the purpose of this report to offer teachers from junior high through college a brief handbook on the use of oral history in teaching. As subsequent sections will explain, oral history can be successfully adapted to the resources and time dimensions of virtually any teaching situation. A word of caution, however, is in order. Oral history should not be viewed as a panacea that will quickly revitalize the teaching of any subject but rather as a means to improve student motivation by injecting the community into the learning process. Without careful preparation and effective implementation, it can be an educational bust like anything else.

2. A Way to Learn

One of the important pedagogical contributions that oral history can make is to further the understanding of major social studies concepts. Through the use of oral history, the illustrative examples that are used extensively by teachers to facilitate comprehension can be gained locally and by the students themselves. For the imprint of American history can be found in any community whether urban or rural. Students who are given the opportunity to interview family members or community residents about the Great Depression or changing socio-economic conditions in a neighborhood usually develop a far deeper interest in the course because their world and the course material are more fully integrated.

Teachers can also develop their own problems approach by using oral history. Since there are at least two sides to every issue or controversy, and usually more, the experience of examining and resolving such questions can be an invaluable learning situation. Asking students to resolve the discrepancies between textbook and interview accounts about a particular incident or idea is another good way to help them develop critical skills.

The use of oral history in the preparation of a family history paper is still another possible application. It is a truism that every family has a history, but as one old-timer once remarked, "The only trouble with our history is that we pay too little attention to it." Such is the case with most American families. Even when fragments of a family's past are dredged up, it is usually for didactic purposes. It is a rare youth indeed who has not been subjected to a historical lecture on the-way-it-used-to-be. Yet the discovery that the lives of grandparents and parents were shaped by certain major historical trends and events will usually expand the historical consciousness of most students. If students are asked to write a paper dealing with their family in the twentieth century, they can also gain a more meaningful perception of modern America. Furthermore, most families are usually very pleased to have an opportunity to serve as resource persons, and the resulting paper often becomes the official family history.

One of the most significant educational developments to come out of the curricular revolution in the 1960's was the increasing number of courses concerned with the study of local institutions and people. After decades of neglect teachers suddenly began to realize that the study of local history, economics, or sociology could be an excellent way to heighten student interest and convey either the fundamentals or fine points of a discipline. For this type of inquiry, oral history is especially well-suited. Interviews with knowledgeable community residents can often fill major gaps in local sources and also provide a good overview of the important issues that confronted a town or neighborhood. Furthermore, the number of potential local studies is virtually limitless, for often an area's past is shrouded in half-truths and unexamined interpretations. Questions about how local landmarks, customs, and practices originated are all too often answered by remarks like, "I don't know but that's just the way its always been." Through exposure to local history and lore, students usually develop a better understanding if not appreciation of their community or neighborhood. Whether a class is studying the socio-economic influence of a major natural disaster, Prohibition days in the county, the evolution of the pickle industry in North Benton, or the transformation of Friendlyville from a small town to a medium-sized city, oral history can be a useful tool.

The use of oral history to improve interpersonal relations and develop social skills is an application that has only recently begun to receive serious consideration. An incident related to me by a high school teacher effectively underscores the educational potential of this approach. Several years ago a new high school was constructed in upstate Illinois on a tract of land that had once been the property of a nearby farmer. Apparently the old farmer occasionally displayed his resentment over this state of affairs by brandishing a shotgun on his front porch. Derisive shouts and occasional pranks on the part of the students served to further poison the relationship. One semester a teacher decided to take a group of students over to the embattled farmhouse and interview the farmer about the history of the area. After the initial uncertainty of both parties was overcome, the farmer and the students hit it off quite well. The farmer's admission that he had run a good-sized still during Prohibition days on the exact site occupied by the school went a long way toward normalizing relations. In this case the interview removed the stereotyped images held by both sides.

There is no question that the generation gap that is everywhere talked about today has been greatly overemphasized. While certain life-styles associated with the youth rebellion of the 1960's no doubt served to alienate generations from one another, some research indicates that only a small percentage of American youth was ever actively involved.[2] Nevertheless it is true that since age grouping has become so much a part of modern society, young and old have had few chances to communicate. Since generational isolation is particularly hard on adolescents and teenagers who are often groping to find their identity in a confusing world, interviews with older people about growing up or finding a vocation can be a meaningful experience.

One of the primary reasons the wisdom that only comes with age is so often ignored is because many youths have never been taught to be good listeners. Oral history interviewing helps to make good listeners. Sharon Curtin, a noted Virginia writer, admitted recently that she used to earn her Saturday movie money by renting out her grandfather to the neighborhood kids:

> For a dime, they could watch him whittle a chain and a whistle from one piece of birchwood and as a bonus, he would sometimes talk as he whittled. During those lazy, hot afternoons he told stories of Indians and blizzards and how barbed wire ruined the wilderness; he made us hear wolves howl and feel the ground shake as the buffalo stampeded. Week after week, Grandad gave my friends and me the gift of the past.[6]

Almost every teacher who has used oral history in teaching doubtless would agree that the quality of in-class training goes a long way in determining the success or failure of the entire project. This is not to say that every oral history project involving students must be preceeded by a vigorous, semi-professional training process. What is important, however, is that preparatory sessions be tailored to the sophistication of the project. If planning to have students interview grandparents about popular culture in the 1920's, the teacher will probably find a very short training session to be in order. In contrast, a program aimed at accumulating a large collection of interviews on local history would necessitate several weeks of training. The guidelines that follow should be

13

helpful to teachers in planning and conducting training programs. Nevertheless, it is still advisable for interested teachers to experiment with a few interviews themselves so that they can teach from first-hand experience. Like any handbook on how to play tennis or bridge, this report will point out some of the ways to insure good performance but it cannot offer any guarantee of success.

3.   Guidelines for the Interview

The Teacher

An interview is actually nothing more than a purposeful conversation between two people. While there are many different types of interviews such as those used in employment situations and for psychiatric examination, in the case of oral history the purpose of the interview is simply that of information gathering. Unlike the standardized survey interview that social scientists have used so extensively in recent years, the usual oral history interview is an elite or nonstandardized type. Although it is the oral historian who initiates the process and seeks to ask questions in such a way that the information obtained fits into historically meaningful patterns, it is the interviewee who must determine the shape of the interview. In effect the interviewer is merely assisting the narrator in the preparation of a personal memoir.[12]

Under such circumstances no two interviews are ever identical even if the same narrator is interviewed on the same topics by two equally well-trained interviewers. The reason for this is that the outcome of every elite interview is determined in part by the social interaction between the participants. How the interviewer and the interviewee perceive each other psychologically will determine the manner in which questions are asked and responses provided. Every interview thus involves some degree of psychological gaming. The interviewer seeks to draw from the interviewee the fullest possible account while the latter determines (both consciously and unconsciously) whether the former is worthy of this on all topics or something less. It is of course a rare occurrence when an interviewee drops all her/his psychological defenses in an interview situation. The degree of responsiveness and the quality of the information supplied by a willing narrator are thus determined by the knowledge, skill, and personality of the interviewer.[4]

Because of the vagaries of long-term memory, the interviewer is always cast in the role of an explorer constantly probing for richer caches of information. This is a necessity since the ability to recount events that occurred a quarter or half century ago seems to be more dependent upon the personality of an individual than on the purely physiological dimensions of memory.[10] The maxim of Herodotus is most appropriate in this regard, "If ye expect not the unexpected, ye shall not find truth." Put in more contemporary terms by the noted historian, Daniel Aaron: the oral historian ". . . resembles rather a hunter stalking his unpredictable quarry in a jungle. . . . What starts out looking like a rabbit may turn into a porcupine. . . ."[1]

Before offering some pointers on interviewing itself a few comments are in order on the subject of equipment. For reasons of economy and convenience, the cassette recorder is the type that is generally used in most student-centered oral history projects, because few fledgling projects have sufficient funds to purchase new equipment and must rely upon whatever is locally available. For example, in about one half of the high school courses reported on in the 1974 survey, "The Use of Oral History in teaching,"[13] the students actually supplied their own recorders. For all practical purposes, the quality and type of recorders used will always be determined by the goals of the project, availability of funds, and the degree of conversancy with recording equipment that a teacher attains.

Oral history interviews also vary in terms of the nature of the information sought. This in turn has a direct bearing on the type of relationship that develops between the interviewer and the interviewee. The autobiographical type of interview wherein the main purpose is to secure a complete life history of an individual usually necessitates a long series of interviews. The greater familiarity resulting from such an interview situation is especially advantageous. In contrast, the more common topic or subject type often involves only one or two interviews with an individual. Such interviews usually focus on one important aspect or period of a person's life. These may range from the war experiences of a retired teacher to the logging camp remembrances of an old woodsman. Although the rapport that an interviewer can build up in this type of interview may be less substantial than in the autobiographical situation, the economy of the topic interview in terms of focus and person-hours makes it far more practical for most programs. This is likewise applicable to a related type, the biographical interview. This is a selective interview as well. It involves nothing more than an individual's recollection of an important historical figure like a former president or mayor.

Although almost all oral historians view the one-to-one interview as an article of faith, a number of teachers have experimented successfully with student interview teams. This approach provides the social reassurance that many junior high and some senior high school students need to overcome their fears about interviewing people whom they do not know. While it can be argued that the presence of multiple interviewers may perplex the narrator and lessen the quality of the oral memoir, teachers should weigh this potential disadvantage against the practical variables of class size, availability of tape recorders, and student attitudes.

The Interviewer

Like any skill, whether academic or athletic, there are no hard and fast rules that will guarantee success. In a recent article Amelia Fry, a pioneer in the field, underscored this point by systematically debunking certain rules of the game that she had earlier set forth.[9] Despite this *caveat* oral historians are in general agreement that certain ground rules will help to insure a successful experience for those who participate.

The following guidelines are particularly appropriate for students.

1. In making the initial contact with a prospective interviewee, care should be exercised that a clear presentation is made of the purpose and nature of the interview. Such explanations need not be lengthy but should inform the prospective interviewee of the general areas to be covered, how the interview will be conducted, and what will be done with the information supplied.

2. Student interviewers should have a sound general knowledge of the subject or topics to be explored. If, for example, a student plans to interview a retired police officer about how the local department has changed since the 1930's, the student should do enough background reading to have some idea of the major national trends. Such preparation is necessary to secure full educational benefits from the use of oral history. Without any background a student interviewer cannot ask the types of questions that will elicit the most important information. In a similar vein, the unprepared student does not qualify as an active learner, which is one of the basic justifications for the exercise.

17

3. Interviews should not begin abruptly. Ideally students should have a preliminary visit with an interviewee to gather biographical information and establish initial rapport. In most school situations, however, such visits may be an unaffordable luxury. Where this is true, the student should spend the first few minutes in general conversation before formally beginning the interview. The social nature of every interview makes breaking the ice an essential prerequisite.

4. Oral historians ordinarily rely on broad-gauge questions. This is not to say that questions that require a yes or no answer may not be useful at times, but generally the how, what, where, and why queries elicit the best responses. This is true because the most successful oral history interviews involve long monologues on the part of the narrator. Whenever an interview becomes a dialogue, one can be sure that something has gone wrong.

5. Oral historians must be active listeners. The interviewer should be able to monitor the quality of what an interviewee is relating while also listening for clues or inferences that may reveal new areas worth exploring. The art of active listening must be developed, and if an interviewer feels drained following an hour-long session this is a good indication that she/he is developing the skill.

6. Interviewers should guard against becoming so enamored of an interviewee that they forfeit their objectivity. In other words interviewers must be supportive but not supine. This is necessary because one is seeking the narrator's account so that it can become a source just like a personal letter or diary. Such balance is especially hard for young interviewers to achieve.

7. If an interviewee appears to be deliberately laying it on a little thick or presenting a very distorted account, the interviewer can switch to a negative tack without damaging rapport. An interviewer can simply state that other sources she/he has consulted have taken an opposite view and then see what the narrator's reaction is. Skeptical comments by the interviewer may accomplish the same purpose but with more risk. In the same vein, tough questions about sensitive subjects often secure the best responses midway through the interview after the interviewee has become more trusting and relaxed.

8. Note-taking during an interview is usually helpful. Scratching on a notepad provides a convenient and unobtrusive outlet for nervousness. By jotting down new questions as they come to

mind and names whose spelling is uncertain, the interviewer can insure both accuracy and thoroughness. After the interview has ended, the interviewer can ask the narrator for the correct spellings thus saving considerable time if and when a transcript or index is prepared.

9. Interviewers should refrain from asking compound questions. Such an approach can be very disheartening to an interviewee. Another common mistake made by student interviewers is rushing the narrator to respond. This can be done in a number of ways but usually involves rephrasing a question several times because the narrator did not respond immediately. Students need only be reminded of how confusing it is for them to be asked a difficult question in class and then, when they fail to answer at once, to have the teacher rephrase the question again and again. Since they were uncertain about the initial question (perhaps with good reason), the barrage of subsequent questions only befuddles them and usually results in pained silence.

10. Difficulties concerning the use of tape recorders are most often the fault of the interviewer. If the interviewer is nervous about the operation of a tape recorder, this can have a negative effect on the interview itself. Students should receive thorough training in the care and use of tape recorders. A pre-test of the tape recorder and tape before arriving on the scene for an interview should be standard procedure.

11. Within a few days after an interview has been recorded, the interviewer should listen to the entire tape. This can be especially helpful to students in improving their interview technique. This procedure also enables the interviewer to prepare for the next interview and to formulate good follow-up questions.

12. In situations where more than one interview is conducted with a particular interviewee, it is helpful to begin the second and all subsequent interviews with important follow-up questions. If the length of time between interviews is relatively short, the interviewee oftentimes has thought of additional information which can best be presented at the beginning of the next interview.

13. Since significant collections of snapshots and more formal photographs are the most abundant and easily usable historical record found in the average American family, they can be of assistance to oral historians. Pictures of important events or individuals can often improve the memory of a narrator. The use

of iconographic materials can also make the oral history project more worthwhile for the students involved. One word of caution, however, is in order. Unless students are able to determine prior to an interview which photographs are of historical interest, interviews using this approach can become long, disjointed monologues about highly personal and perhaps trivial family affairs.

14. It is a rare occurrence when an interview is completed without some degree of digression. Since the trail that an interview follows is not always well-marked, this is understandable. If a narrator continually lapses into prolonged digressions about unrelated matters despite the best efforts of the student to get them back to the topic at hand, the student should subsequently seek another interviewee.

15. A good interviewer according to Lewis Dexter has "as many of the virtues as possible of a good social scientist, a good reporter and a good historian."[7] Put in more colloquial terms by Amelia Fry, the interviewer "should be that combination of journalist-historian, the Grand Inquisitor, Mata Hari, Sherlock Holmes, and, one might add, Vanderbilt and Mellon."[9] Since no living oral historian has yet fulfilled either definition, why not give your students a crack at it?

The Interviewee

While the preceding section was addressed to the interviewers, a word need be said about interviewees and their selection. The vast majority of all interviews that have been conducted by oral historians since 1948 have been with the elderly. Unless a Florida promoter actually locates the fabled fountain of youth in the near future, the aged will probably continue to be the prime subjects of oral historians. This is of course a natural outgrowth of the relatively recent emergence of oral history and the practical determination of most programs to gather memoirs from individuals who have the shortest life expectancy. The adage "the older the better," however, should not be the only basis for selecting interviewees for educationally oriented projects. If oral history is used in conjunction with a unit on the 1960's, then Viet Nam veterans, former McCarthy campaign workers, and liberated women might be potential interviewees. Along similar lines the study of neighborhood or community changes since World War II could involve interviews with people from all age groups.

A request to be interviewed for whatever purpose is generally flattering to an individual. Even prominent individuals in a community are not usually above this reaction. Although simple curiosity often leads a person to consent to an interview initially, an interview request also signifies that a person's life experiences have meaning for others. In a similar vein an interview represents an invitation to teach. Since most people tend to be natural-born teachers about the things they know best, such an opportunity is rarely refused.

The interviewer must always be sensitive to the interviewee's personal stake in the interview and avoid any psychological harm. Interviewers who continually ask very detailed factual questions, for example, may make the narrator feel inadequate. This can be a very shattering experience to an older person who is anxious to prove her/his worth. Interviewees can also be disconcerted by rapid topical or chronological shifts in questioning. The oral historian should always try to stay within the prearranged boundaries that have been set for the interview. Finally, students should be made to realize that narrators are not simply talking books. Unlike a book, which provides the necessary information to anyone using the table of contents or index, interviewees deserve special handling.

Summary

The noted American historian, Carl Becker, once wrote that every man is his own historian.[3] Although this may be the case, everyone is certainly not an oral historian. Certain students as well as adults may not be willing to conduct interviews, but most oral history projects can be organized to provide meaningful learning experiences for the noninterviewers as well. In the Foxfire Project such a division of labor has worked very successfully. Students doing research, transcribing or editing tapes are making important contributions to any oral history project.

There is no time-honored method for training students to become oral historians. The suggestions that follow represent a distillation of training methods used in various programs.

1. Oral history by its very nature does not readily lend itself to the lecture method. Training sessions of whatever depth and length should involve maximum student participation.
2. The importance of the tape recorder can be easily demonstrated by casually telling the class a story one day and asking them to

write down the story from memory the next. The general inaccuracy of their recall together with the glaring discrepancies between various accounts will be enough to convince even the most stubborn student that a tape recorder is essential to oral history interviewing.

3. If you or one of your colleagues has experimented with oral history, the resulting tapes can be played for the class to demonstrate some of the preferred techniques as well as the common problems. If locally compiled tapes are not available, you may be able to borrow or purchase tapes from larger oral history programs in your state or region.

4. Once the students have gained a rudimentary conception of oral history, they should be given the opportunity to put their knowledge into practice. Short interviews with family members or schoolmates will help students gain experience. The in-class evaluation of such interviews will be beneficial to all.

5. While any type of interviewing lends itself to deep psychological evaluation, such an approach with students— even on the college level—may tend to stifle their natural curiosity by making them overly self-conscious. This can severely retard their development as interviewers. Periodic class discussions of interview techniques, once the project is underway, is an excellent way to maintain and improve student skills.

6. In cases where an oral history project is continued from one class to another, students who participated in the first phase may be useful in training subsequent classes. Peer status and the immediacy of their experiences often enable selected students to effectively assist neophytes in learning the art of oral history.

7. Every effort should be made by the teacher to sit down with students after their first interview experience and evaluate the results. Positive reinforcement at this time is very important since even the most self-confident individuals are often unable to determine how it went. This unique form of instant replay also helps students to better understand their strong and weak points and to go on from there.

8. To help students formulate effective questions, some teachers prepare lists of topics to cover in an interview. This is especially helpful for junior high students. A sample topic sheet can be found in Chapter 5.

4. Uses of the Tape

The question of what to do after the tapes come in is a very valid one. While students hopefully will learn a great deal from the actual interview experience itself, the resulting tapes can be valuable learning resources as well. Since oral history tapes are primary sources, they fit well into the inquiry method as previously noted. Having students check available written sources to corroborate important accounts and observations provided by interviewees is an excellent way to develop critical skills. Segments drawn from particularly dramatic or revealing interviews can also be used to highlight related text material. Short oral biographies and slide-tape presentations can be developed by students using representative segments drawn from interviews. Finally, a collection of the best interviews recorded over the years will be a continuing resource for a department or division.

For research-minded oral historians, the written transcript of an interview is considered the most important product. Until recently the Oral History Research Office at Columbia University as well as other major collections retained only selected tapes. In the case of oral history projects involving students, the transcription of interviews necessitates much more supervision on the part of the teacher as well as increased amounts of class time. This is not to say that the experience of transcribing and editing an interview is not an excellent learning experience. It simply demands a great deal more from all parties concerned.

There are a number of differing schools of thought on the subject of transcribing. Some oral historians take a purist view and seek to attain a verbatim transcript of the interview. They argue that to do otherwise is to tamper with primary sources in a manner reminiscent of the nineteenth century historian Jared Sparks who tiddied up George Washington's correspondence. Most oral historians favor limited editing of the transcript so that the interview is more readable in written form. This usually involves eliminating false starts, redundent oral sounds, and tightening up the language structure. Since interviewees speak differently than they write, such editing is often essential to avoid undue embarrassment to the source.

The preparation of a brief, topical index for each interview and an ongoing, general index for the entire collection represents another preservation alternative. Such indexes essentially provide a table of contents for each tape. By means of the digital counter found on most cassette recorders, the interviewer can note with reasonable accuracy the location on the tape of the narrator's remarks on various general topics. A card file can then be assembled containing a general index to guide interested students to the tapes that contain information on such topics as a local ethnic group or Korean War experiences. Although this approach is a far less efficient and a more cumbersome means of storing and retrieving information from oral history sources, it is much less expensive and time-consuming than transcription. A sample tape index is included in the next chapter.

The information gained through oral history interviews must never be treated lightly. Caution should always be exercised so that oral history accounts do not find their way into local gossipvines. Although most interviews focus on events that transpired twenty to forty or fifty years in the past, in small communities especially, careless use of sensitive information may wreck the project. Good sense will usually dictate the right course. If you plan to permanently retain tapes and/or transcripts for the purpose of building a living history center for your social studies department or local historical society, then a legal release agreement should be used. This is simply a safeguard which most oral historians use to protect themselves against any subsequent change of heart or mind on the part of an interviewee or interviewee's family. A sample release agreement is included in the next chapter.

5. Developing an Oral History Project: A Sample

Sample Discussion Areas for the Interview

An important preliminary consideration for the interviewer is to decide what will be discussed. The following list includes many of the basic subject areas that most interviews cover. This list does not exhaust all possibilities but should help direct both student and teacher.

SUBJECTS TO COVER IN EACH INTERVIEW°

1. Childhood Days—Name and birthplace of parents; number and names of brothers and sisters; age. Land owned by parents; what happened to land; how was it divided. Family life; other childhood memories of what life was like; any remarriages of parents; where brothers and sisters now live; family reunions. Did they grow own food? If so, what? Do they remember periods of scarcity of food? If born in another area, when did they move and how?

2. Schooling—Amount parents had; amount brothers and sisters got; schools and teachers; other students; settlement schools; ways schools have changed.

°From Appalachian Oral History Project, 1970. Alice Lloyd College, Lees Junior College, Emory & Henry College, and Appalachian State University. Reprinted with permission.

3. **Occupations of Interviewee**—housewife, logger, doctor, farmer, merchant, teacher, pharmacist. List all jobs person has worked at and when they worked; when did they have hardest time finding a job; how has the work which they know changed over the years?

4. **Religion**—What sort of churches were in the area? To which did most people in their community belong? What were they like and how have they changed?

5. **Community**—How did it get its name? How and why was it formed in the first place? Major events and activities affecting the community. How has the community changed over the years? Who have been the community decision-makers? What made them the community leaders? Are there minority groups in the community? If so, what group(s) and how have relations been with them? Were some families poorer than others? Did others look out for them? How many people lived in the community? Has population changed greatly? If so, when and why? Where did they go?

6. **Politics**—Any memories of specific elections—local, state or federal. Political leaders in their particular community. How did people tend to vote and why. How has the politics changed over the years? Information about local politicians.

7. **Transportation**—How did people get around? Where did the roads and railroads run? When were the railroads built? When did the first automobiles come in?

8. **Crafts and Customs**—Soapmaking, curing, weaving, chairmaking, local cures, making molasses; searching for ginseng, May apple, and snakeroot; courtin then and now; others.

9. **Law Officers and Badmen**—Prohibition, pre-twentieth century, the Depression; Black Bart train robber.

10. **Folktales, Legends, and Superstitions.**

11. **Union Organizing**—When did the union come in? Was it recognized or did it have to fight for recognition? Strikes, with dates. Who were local union leaders? Any memories of national leaders or union organizers. Information on the AFL—how it works, how many men were in it, the quality of the leadership, internal struggles, etc.

12. **Music**—Ballads, songs—encourage interviewees to sing or play a musical instrument if they seem interested.

13. **Depressions**—1907 and 1930 and LOCAL HARD TIMES.

14. **Wars**—Any relatives in Civil War? Recollections of Spanish-American War, World War I, World War II, Korean War, and Viet Nam.

Sample Release Form

Another important preliminary consideration is obtaining permission to use an interview. Oral historians are strong believers in the adage, "An ounce of prevention is worth a pound of cure." By means of this simple precaution, a teacher can insure the integrity and continuity of a project. A sample release form is presented here to show what it should include.

CARTHAGE COLLEGE ORAL HISTORY PROJECT
2001 Alford Drive
Kenosha, Wisconsin

I hereby give and grant to the Carthage College Oral History Project my tape recorded memoir as a donation for such scholarly and educational purposes as the Project shall determine. It is expressly understood that the full literary rights of this memoir pass to the Carthage College Oral History Project and that no rights whatsoever are to vest in my heirs now or at my death.

_____

Signature of narrator

_____

Address of narrator

_____

Signature of interviewer

_____

Address of interviewer

_____

Date of agreement

_____

Subject of Tape(s)

Sample Transcript

Transcripts are more accessible than tapes because one can read a transcript without the aid of a machine. Consequently, oral history in its final form is most frequently written. One way for students to become familiar with the technique of transcribing interviews is to examine actual transcripts. What follows is the transcript of the first part of an interview.

NICHOLAS WADE

ON

KENOSHA AT THE TURN OF THE CENTURY

AND

Recreation

Crime

Health Care

Eating Habits

Irish Population

By
JOHN NEUENSCHWANDER
On June 14, 1973
At Nicholas Wade's Real Estate Office
Editor
John Vogt

Completed, June 26, 1974

Restrictions, None

CARTHAGE COLLEGE
ORAL HISTORY PROJECT

The following autobiographical interview was held on June 14, 1973, with Mr. Nicholas Wade, a Studebaker dealer, City Councilman and Realtor. The interview was conducted in the Real Estate Office of Mr. Nicholas Wade. The interviewer is John Neuenschwander, Director of the Carthage College Oral History Project.

JN: Tell us a little bit about your family and then your growing up years in Kenosha.

NW: Well, my grandparents came from England in 1843, or '44, and he served in the Civil War. After he came back from there, there was the large fire in Chicago, and he went down there to help rebuild. While he was there he fell off some scaffolding and broke his neck and died.

JN: The Chicago fire of 1877?

NW: That's right. Then my dad was left with the rest of the family; him being the youngest, he was shoved around for a while from farm to farm. After he married, why—they had twelve children, they lost six when they were real young—and there was six of them that lived. Now there's my sister and myself left out of the family. I was born on what we called Grant Street in the City of Kenosha—now it's Sixth Avenue. I started school in the Stewart Building (it was used for a meat market and then finally for a school) on Bronson Street which is now 43rd Street. As I recall, when I was about six years old, we lived in the county with all the little kids that went to school there. My Dad and my brothers cleaned up the pastures. We had ten acres out there where the Jefferson School is today—across from Washington Bowl, in fact it joined Washington Bowl. The morning of the picnic I went to school and was going to lead the kids out to the home, and after we got to the Northwestern tracks, a freight train came along and all the little kids got scared and run home. We had about ten gallons of lemonade that my mother made, but we never did have a picnic. The swings were up and everything, but we never did have the picnic. At that time the Northwestern tracks were the city limits. As far as that was concerned the North Limits was down about 38th Street.

JN: Do you know why your grandmother and grandfather came to the United States? Why they left England?

NW: Well, it could have been possible that my grandfather married a pretty well-to-do family there—a family by the name of Stone—but we never did get the true facts. It was the Stone family and at the time we were under the impression that it was the family that made the "Chinaware" in England. A history of the family—in fact father sent over to England, to what we call the County Clerk here in order to find more information. That man even went out to the cemetery and checked to see what there was to the family history there. My Father sent the man in England a 5 or 10 dollar bill.

JN: Your grandfather came to Kenosha and he went right into farming then?

NW: Oh no, he was a carpenter.

JN: Carpenter?

NW: Yeah—he built quite a few homes that are standing now on the north side here (on 46th Street—8th Avenue).

JN: Did you ever find out how he happened to come to Kenosha?

NW: No, I didn't—we never did find out how he happened to settle here.

JN: What occupation was your father in?

NW: My dad was a carpenter. He did a lot of carpenter work for building homes. I recall when I carried dinner to him on one job on Pleasant Street, then you used to slack your own plaster. It looked so nice to step in and I was barefooted so I stepped into it. I thought it was solid and I stepped into it. I was going to wipe off my feet when my dad and uncle both came sailing from the house and grabbed me and used sand, because the lime would have eaten the flesh off the bottom of my feet. They both did carpenter work and then in later years naturally he retired, but we had good parents. We were poor
. . .

JN: What kind of standing did you feel, as you were growing up, that your family had in the community with your father being a carpenter? Working class people?

NW: No—that's right. Those days were different than today. If there was a fire and they wanted volunteers for it, he'd go and help. He was very good, and mother was very good. You see, in our day the situation was different than today. When neighbors were sick, there was no question about religion or anything else, Mother would make a bowl of soup and take it to the neighbor—she'd even get up in the morning and get us off to school and then go over and get the neighbor's children off to school. The neighbor would do the same. There was a big difference then. I remember when I was a little guy and a neighbor came over and needed $10 for his taxes and Dad said, "Give it to him." The neighbor said, "I'll give you a note." and Dad said, "Your note's no good if your word's no good." There was no such thing as taking a note or anything of the kind. I recall too when we were kids we talked about kind friends. If I was given a dime or quarter to go to the store to get the groceries of some kind and accidentally dropped it in a crack in the wooden sidewalk that was the last of that. Some of the fellows wouldn't allow you to pull your dime out of the sidewalk. I don't know, we lived much different then. We used to make our own fun. We'd go to the electric light and we'd play there. There was a 9:00 curfew. You'd see fellows scatter in all different directions to get home before the police would come around. We respected things then, see—it's different than today. Kids don't give a darn today. Of course, we didn't have much to do. All we'd do was get up in the morning and have breakfast, take the cows and drive them to pasture and then come back home, wash up and go to school. At 11:30 I'd get out (school didn't get out till 12:00, but I'd get out at 11:30) run home, get the dinner buckets and take them to Simmons. Then I'd eat with my dad. Then I'd go back to school. As soon as school was out, I'd go home, change clothes, trot out to get the cow in the pasture, get her back home, settle her down, feed the chickens and if there was some potato bugs to be picked we'd pick the potato bugs. Then after we had our supper dad would say, "If you're finished with your lessons, go out and play." At 9:00 you were home. See, like I say, we made our own fun and we had a lot of fun in the short time that we had.

JN: What sort of make-fun games did you have?

NW: Well—we played long baseball with that picnic ball, and we would box under the lights; of course we played "run sheep, run" (you know what that is, don't you?).

JN: I recall the name, but I can't describe it.

NW: Well, you start out you have a bunch on one side and a bunch on the other side. Then this one bunch would count up to 100. You'd start out and take a piece of chalk, they were wooden sidewalks and you would mark them which direction you ran in, and the case where you would fool them on your direction. You'd chase around about 6–7 blocks and come back to the starting place. There were so many different things. Now you take these little kids—when someone got married, we'd have a shivaree. You have two older boys—one would have a clarinet and one would have a trombone and maybe another would have drums and we'd go and shivaree them. That's what we called it. Dad made an outfit. It's like a ringer and you get a lot of noise out of it. Some days the fellow would come out and give you a dollar bill. The older fellows would have an eighth of beer. There were eighths in those days. We just went along for the fun. We had a lot of fun, but we never did drink any beer. That we weren't allowed to do until we were 21. We lived with my sister, near Jefferson School, until she straightened things out there after her husband passed away. We used to walk from there, my brother John and I, with two pails of milk which we delivered. Elson had a store on 43rd Street and we delivered milk to him on our way to school. We hiked from there to school and you can imagine what the kids today would say if they hiked from there to school. It did us a lot of good. I say that the work that we did in our younger days built up our bodies and I don't think there's any question about it but that it was good.

JN: When you were growing up in Kenosha, did you hear anything about Zalmon G. Simmons and what he meant to the city or anything?

NW: Sure—we knew him. He was very nice and he did a lot of good things for the city. In fact practically all of the people on the North Side worked for him. See, there was the Simmons Plant and they used to have boats come in, sailboats, with oak lumber for crates. Crates to crate the beds up in. If the boat was coming in and there was a north-eastern up they would have to throw out thousands of feet of lumber in order to make the harbor. The whole top deck they would throw out. Well, the people would wait until that lumber would come into shore and then they would go and get it. They would build chicken coops out of it, also barns and whatnot. American Motors has that old Simmons plant now, but before the whole freight yard right up to the dock was all lumber piles. Also the Bain Wagon Works was right there on 55th Street. After automobiles came out, it kind of put the wagon works out of business.

JN: The whole North Side worked at Simmons or Bain Wagon Works? Was this largely the German element?

NW: Practically all. The Irish settled on the South and West Side. Later on the Italian folks came in.

JN: What type of neighborhood did you live and grow up in, in terms of ethnic groups and religion?

NW: There was quite a few Protestants. There were more Protestants than Catholics at that time. That didn't matter. Like I told you in the first place, everybody helped everybody. It was not a case of dog-eat-dog like today. Yes, I finished school at St. George's when I was about 14 years old and went to work.

JN: This would amount to the end of primary school or junior high school?

NW: No—I never went that high. When I was 14—in those days the judge would give you a permit to go to work—I went to work out at what they called the Chicago-Kenosha Hosiery, on 24th and 60th. I worked there for a short time, until I went to work for my cousin in the meat market. I worked 19 years in the meat market and then I went into real estate in 1919. In 1932 I went in the automobile business.

JN: How would you contrast the meat business, when you were in it, with the meat business today?

NW: You mean when we were selling pork steak for 8 or 9 cents a pound?

JN: Not just the price, but the way you conducted your business, handled your meat and so on.

NW: Well, we probably spent more time in the market than they do today. Because, to start off with, you got up at 5:00 in the morning, went over to the barn, fed the horses, cleaned them and hitched them up. We went out and took orders. When you finished, about 11 o'clock, I'd go home for lunch, get back and the rest of them would take off for lunch. The first thing we had to do at my cousin's market was to clean up the blocks, the counters, and the scales. Then we'd cut up a round or two and get things ready for the afternoon trade. Then when you got that done, you rolled your sleeves up and went out into the icebox, a great big icebox. You have a great big tub of meat out there, which has seasoned three or four days for sausage. You stuffed the sausage, then started a fire under your kettle, and started a fire in the smokehouse. You

33

smoked the sausage and put it in the kettle. When you finished you took it out, hung it up to dry, then put it in the icebox. Usually you finished about 7:00 in the evening.

JN: So the morning was usually devoted to taking orders and the afternoon was a delivery period.

NW: No, no, mornings were delivery, too. If you came late with a piece of roast beef or a piece of soup meat, some of these old Germans would tell you that you had to be there on time.

JN: Were there different cuts of meat then than are today?

NW: No, the same. We killed our own poultry, all of it: chickens, geese, turkey, and ducks. My cousin never would buy any barrels of chickens or anything like that. You knew that they were all fresh. The same way with meat. It had to be first class or we didn't cut it. The cuts were the same. Maybe there's a different name for what we call plate or brisket, but outside of that the same. You take steaks, they were about 15 or 16 cents a pound and today they're a $1.70. That's the difference.

Sample Tape Index

Preparing an index rather than a transcript is an easier though less complete method of storing information from each tape. The following tape index illustrates how to order information for quick retrieval.

Interview I with Robert Henry
February 18, 1975
by
Angela Zophy

Tape I, side 1

0-11	Silence.
12-	Refers to George Epstein's collection of Kenosha History.
85-	Earliest childhood memories of the Old Howe Building.
143-	Recalls Feathertown Mattress factory fire.

185-	Early methods of butchering meat (do it yourself type).
310-	Schools attended.
360-	Water sources and sewage customs.
386-	Livery stable and its neighborhood (livery was family business).
422-	Old Malt House explosion and fire.
459-	Durkee School memories and the dedication of Simmons Library. Side 1 ends at 477.

Side 2

480-	Livery business, Old Farmer's Market.
500-	Barter system between farmers and town grocers.
528-	Credit arrangements, cost of living.
600-	First hospital in Kenosha, Pleasant Prairie Powder Mill explosion, loss of life therein; care of aged.
655-	Kenosha roads and streets (condition of).
676-	Trolley and pranksters.
735-	Alderman O'Brien's confrontation with "Big Mary" (tavern owner).
782-	Main street maintenance problems, descriptions.
816-	New Year's Eve celebration customs.
837-	Dance clubs as social entertainment. Side 2 ends at 857.

6. Conclusion

There is an old saying that "History repeats itself because no one was listening the first time."[14] Whether oral history will ever invalidate this maxim is a moot point, but as a teaching aid it can offer students an opportunity to learn directly from their community by turning local human resources into course materials. For the local community has always been a potential laboratory where students could discover and test ideas. Unfortunately, it has rarely been used to its fullest capacity. Oral history is one means by which teachers can tap this educational resource. The study of important modern developments like the Great Depression, suburbanization, and the ecology crisis can seem otherworldly to many students if their only knowledge of these events and conditions comes from textbooks and other non-direct sources. A chief use of oral history then is to relate students' personal worlds to local surroundings and society at large.

Although to some, oral history may appear to be a radical departure from conventional pedagogy, in reality, it is a very old method of teaching. In a society that is becoming increasingly technocratic and impersonal, the need for such an intensely human way to learn is obvious. For this reason alone, oral history should become an educational mainstay in the years ahead.

References

References

1. Aaron, Daniel. "The Treachery of Recollection: The Inner and the Outer History." *Essays on History and Literature.* (Edited by Robert Bremner.) Columbus: Ohio State University Press, 1966. pp. 7–26.
2. Adelson, Joseph. "What Generation Gap?" *The Character of Americans* (Edited by Michael McGiffert.) Homewood, Ill.: Dorsey Press, 1970. pp. 378–88.
3. Becker, Carl. *Every Man His Own Historian.* N.Y.: Crofts, 1935. 325 pp.
4. Bingham, Walter Van Dyke, and Moore, Bruce Victor. *How to Interview.* Fourth edition. N.Y.: Harper and Row, 1959. 277 pp.
5. Colman, Gould P. "Oral History—An Appeal for More Systematic Procedures." *The American Archivist* 28:79–83; Jan. 1965.
6. Curtin, Sharon. "The Value of Old Folks at Home." *The Milwaukee Journal* 26–29; Jan. 6, 1974.
7. Dexter, Lewis Anthony. *Elite and Specialized Interviewing.* Evanston, Ill.: Northwestern University Press, 1970. 205 pp.
8. Dixon, Elizabeth I., and Mink, James, editors. *Oral History at Arrowhead: The Proceedings of the First National Colloquium on Oral History.* Los Angeles: Oral History Association, 1967. pp. 1–95.
9. Fry, Amelia R. "The Nine Commandments of Oral History." *Journal of Library History* 3:63–73; Jan. 1968.
10. Howe, Michael J.A. *Introduction to Human Memory: A Psychological Approach.* N.Y.: Harper and Row, 1970. 113 pp.
11. Meckler, Alan, and McMullin, Ruth, editors. *Oral History Collections.* N.Y.: R.R. Bowker Co., 1975. 344 pp.
12. Morrissey, Charles. "On Oral History Interviewing." *Elite and Specialized Learning.* (Lewis Anthony Dexter.) Evanston, Ill.: Northwestern University Press, 1970. pp. 111–18.
13. For complete results of this survey, see: Neuenschwander, John; Mathews, Johnye; and Charlton, Tom. "The Use of Oral History in Teaching: A Report on the 1974 Survey." *The Oral History Review* 1975.
14. Szasz, Ferenc M. "The Many Meanings of History, Part III." *The History Teacher* 8:208–17. Feb. 1975.
15. Whittemore, Reed. "Review of *The Foxfire Book II.*" *The New Republic* 168:26; June 23, 1973.
16. Wigginton, Eliot. "Oral History as a Teaching Tool." *The Oral History Review* 30–35; 1973.

Annotated Bibliography

Annotated Bibliography

Baum, Willa K. *Oral History for the Local Historical Society.* Revised edition. Nashville: American Association for State and Local History, 1971.

This is the first how-to-do-it pamphlet ever published and it is still the best.

Cash, Joseph A. *The Practice of Oral History.* New York: Microfilming Corporation, 1975.

A thoughtful account of how oral history is practiced in South Dakota.

Meckler, Alan M., and McCullin, Ruth, editors. *Oral History Collections.* New York: R. R. Bowker Company, 1975.

This is the definitive guide to both oral history source materials and programs in the U.S.A. and abroad.

Moss, William W. *Oral History Program Manual.* New York: Praeger Publishers, 1974.

An excellent account of the concepts and practices of the oral history program at the John F. Kennedy Library, Waltham, Massachusetts.

Shumway, Gary L., and Hartley, William G. *An Oral History Primer.* Published by the authors, 1973.

A more recent how-to-do-it pamphlet which contains some good tips on interviewing.

Terkel, Studs, *Envelopes of Sound: Six Practitioners Discuss the Method, Theory and Practice of Oral History and Oral Testimony*. New York: Precedent Publishers, 1975.

This anthology contains a number of very thoughtful articles on the state of the field including a very revealing interview with the nation's most famous oral historian, Studs Terkel.

Waserman, Manfred J. *Bibliography on Oral History*. New York: The Oral History Association, 1971.

Although it needs to be updated, this is the basic guide to all works on or related to oral history.

Wilkie, James W. *Elitelore*. Los Angeles: University of California Press, 1973.

A provocative essay on studying self-perceptions of Latin American leaders through oral history interviewing.